In
memory
of your beloved
♡ Cat ♡ -
the who
paw prints will remain
on your heart -
forever -

For Every Cat An Angel

written and illustrated by
Christine Davis

For Every Cat An Angel

Printed in China

Lighthearted Press Inc.
P.O. Box 90125
Portland, OR 97290
www.lightheartedpress.com

ISBN-13: 978-0-9659225-1-7
ISBN-10: 0-9659225-1-0

20 19 18 17 16

From the author.....

For as long as I can remember I was connected to fur, but that fur was always connected to a dog! It was not until later in my life that I began to make space for the mysterious feline I felt was out there.... somewhere.... looking for me.

It was my beloved dog, Jake, who discovered the litter of kittens under the deck. He invited them in to become part of the family for he, too, had once been homeless. Dickens, Pippen, Molly and Star immediately took over my home...and Jake's bed. My tireless dog brooded over his feline charges, licking the formula off of their faces and nosing them back if they wandered too far. But it was my life that had been changed forever. I didn't know there were four empty places in my heart that only these little furballs could fill. I hadn't realized how much I needed a feline fairy Godmother, a role Pippen was destined to fill. I never knew how much fun life could be if you looked at the world through the eyes of a kitten!

I am in awe of these cat creatures. They have cast a spell over me that I don't expect will ever be broken. For those of you who also have been enchanted by cat magic....I offer this little book.

With love and gratitude,
Chris Davis

For Dickens,

Pippen, Molly

and Star,

my forever cats,

who taught

me about

cat magic.

Whenever a kitten is born on earth a guardian angel waits nearby to welcome the kitten into the world and take it under her heavenly wings.

The angel snuggles in close to the kitten, surrounding the bundle of fur with her love. Safely tucked in the angel's arms, the kitten dreams of all the adventures yet to be.

Some want to sing in the midnight cat chorus.

Others dream of long naps in the sun.

Some kittens want to help out in the workplace....
MANAGEMENT POSITIONS ONLY.

BUY CAT FOOD

Whatever path the kitten chooses, it will always be loved by its guardian angel.

Kittens have the enchanting gift of captivating all who come in contact with them...even guardian angels! You will often find them playing together, batting at butterflies just passing by.

As the kitten grows older it begins to long for a loving home of its own.

How a person and a cat find each other is very important.

Sometimes a person goes looking for a cat to bring into their family.

Animal Shelter

There are many cats to choose from, but only one that is just right.

And the guardian angel knows her cat will always have toys to pounce on, baskets to hide in and a place on the bed for sleeping at night.

But sometimes an angel knows one special person is waiting for her cat. So she sends the cat through the starry skies until it arrives at the place it is meant to be.

When the person and the ca[t]
find each other something happen[s]
that is just like magic!
They remember they have
been together before,
in a faraway place and
a long ago time. They
will be together
always.

And the
guardian angel looks
down with love,
knowing her cat has found its
forever person and the person
has found their forever cat.

A forever person and their forever cat will share many experiences over a lifetime, like watering flowers and watching the birds.

They will bring each other gifts for no reason at all.

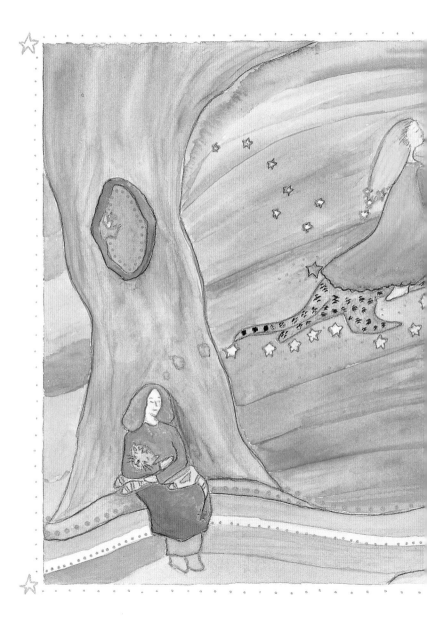

But the
greatest gift
these friends will
share is knowing what is in
the other's heart. The person
understands the wild creature
stalking its prey while it dreams
on her lap. The cat understands the
untamed spirit of the person softly
stroking its fur. And they agree,
as they have before, to keep
their true natures a secret
between them.

A cat can never really be separated from its forever person. Neither time nor space can ever come between them.

So when the cat comes to the end of its earthly life, and must go on ahead without its person beside them, the guardian angel becomes a loving bridge that connects the two friends for as long as the person remains on earth.

Sometimes cats will cross the angel bridge to visit their forever person on earth. You can never be certain where they might turn up.

You may see them in the sky
floating by in a patch of
whipped cream clouds.

Or you might see a familiar shadow
quietly slip by your
Halloween pumpkin.

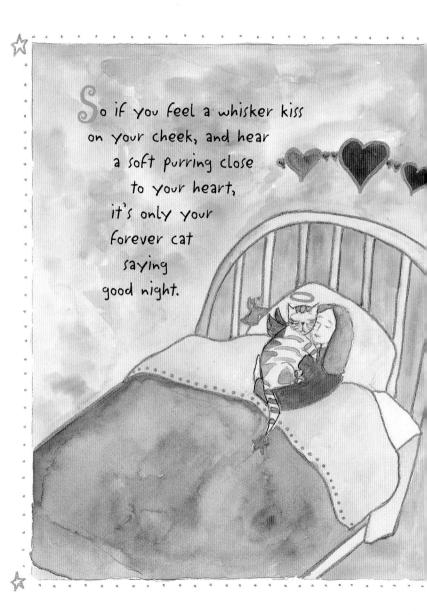

So if you feel a whisker kiss
on your cheek, and hear
a soft purring close
to your heart,
it's only your
forever cat
saying
good night.

Nothing delights your forever cat more than knowing you are happy, even if that means bringing a new kitty into your life. It brings them joy to know another cat will get to share all the love you have to offer. Your forever cat may even stop by to nuzzle the new arrival and let them know they are welcome. So don't be surprised to see your new cat being groomed by an invisible friend...

it probably is!

As the years go by, you and your cat may spend more time napping by the fire.
The day might come when your cat crosses the angel bridge to be with your forever cat and the other animals that had a place in your heart.

One day the angel bridge
will appear to you, and all the
animals you loved on earth will be by
your side to light your way home.

In the middle of all that love your
forever cat will be waiting for you.
        It will be like the day you found
each other on earth. You will know
you have been together before,
  in a far away place
    and a
long ago time,
and nothing
will ever
separate
  you
    again.

And the angels
    will be happy knowing a forever person
        and their forever cat have found
            each other once more.

We hope you enjoyed this
Lighthearted Press book. To order additional copies,
please call our toll free order number 1-877-385-6837
or visit us online at www.lightheartedpress.com.

Books by Christine Davis:

Forever Paws
For Every Dog An Angel
For Every Cat An Angel
The Shelter Dog
Old Dog and the Christmas Wish

Lighthearted Press Inc.
P.O. Box 90125 * Portland, Oregon 97290
503-786-3085 (Phone)
503-786-0315 (Fax)
1-877-385-6837 (Toll free)
www.lightheartedpress.com